Toys around the world

CW00927244

James Dunbar

Children's toys are made in every country in the world. This book will help you find out where some of the famous toys were first made.

You do not have to read the book from beginning to end. Just turn to the pages that interest you.

Contents

Toy houses

Children love to play with toy houses.

⬆ Some children make and paint their own toy houses.

The first dolls' houses were made in Germany.
Now they are made all over the world.
They are often made to look like real houses.

↑ A Spanish dolls' house about one hundred years old.

Toy animals

For hundreds of years children have played with toy animals.

⬆ The buffalo is from the United States of America.
The lion is from China.
The koala bear is from Australia.
The seals are from Norway.

Some of the toys were of wild animals.

Other toys were make believe creatures from fairy tales or festivals.

↥ The snake is from South America.
The kangaroo is from Australia.
The bear is from Russia.

↥ These are Trolls. They are fairy tale creatures from Norway.

Water toys – boats

Children all over the world like to play with toys that float on water.

Boats are made all around the world.
They can be made of wood, plastic or even a coconut shell.

Some boats are not meant to float.
They are models to look at or
to play with on the ground.

This is a very old wooden boat with wheels from Germany.

Water toys – in the bath

Many toys are made for children
to play with at bathtime,
or in a bowl of water.

Some bath toys work when you pour water on them.

Wheeled toys

Some toys have wheels so that you can push or pull them along.

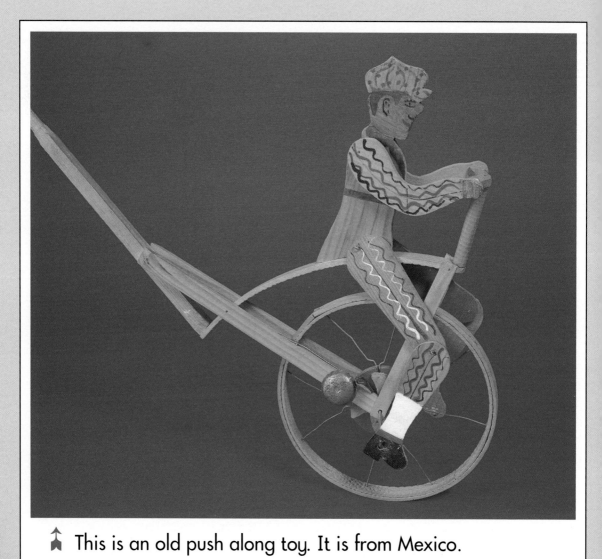

⬆ This is an old push along toy. It is from Mexico.

There are wheels for trains to run on rails.
There are wheels with rubber tyres.
There are bicycle wheels with spokes
and there are caterpillar wheels
which move over rough ground.

All these toys were made in Britain.

Spinning toys

All sorts of toys spin.

Hoops, yoyos and tops all spin in some way.

A hoop is a very old toy from Ancient Greece.
Not many children play with hoops today.

A hoop was made by bending a
thin stick into a circle.

⬆ Yoyos first came from
China. This yoyo is from
Germany.

There are many different sorts of tops.
Many of them come from Japan.

Some tops you spin with your fingers.

Some spin by using string.

Some tops hum when they spin around.

Tops from around the world. Some of them are
better at spinning than others.

Balancing toys

Some toys work by balancing.
A toy balances when the weight
is in the right place.
Mobiles balance in the air,
they hang on a string.

Sometimes there are two equal weights
to help the toy balance.
Some toys balance with one weight
placed on one end of the toy.

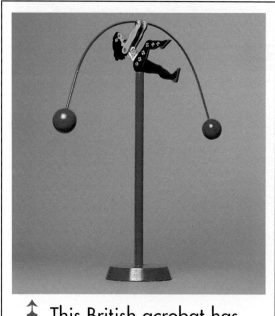

⬆ This British acrobat has
one weight on each side
of the pole.

⬆ This balancing parrot
from Brazil has the
weight in its tail.

🔼 A fish mobile from Thailand.

They balance like a see-saw.
All the weights must be equal.

Puzzles

A puzzle is a thinking game.

Sometimes the game is to put something together in the right way. With other puzzles the game is to find a way of taking them apart.

⬆ Tangram puzzles.

A tangram puzzle comes from China.
It has only seven pieces but it can be put together in hundreds of different ways.
It is difficult to make the seven pieces into a square.

Three wooden jigsaw puzzles. The Kiwi is from New Zealand. The elephant is from Africa. The cats are from Britain.

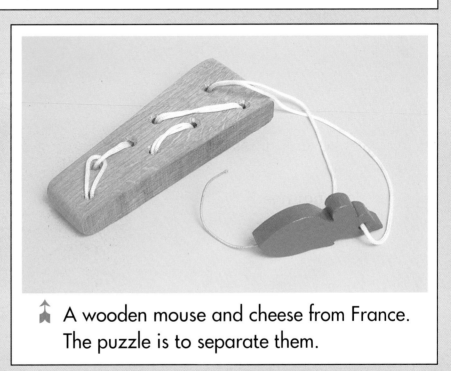

A wooden mouse and cheese from France. The puzzle is to separate them.

Flying toys

Toy aeroplanes and gliders fly in the air.

⬆ This toy aeroplane is Japanese.

Aeroplanes have engines to
make them fly.
A glider does not need an engine.
It needs the wind to keep it
in the air.

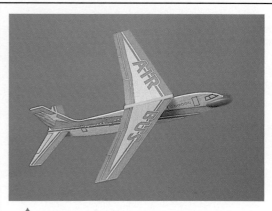

⬆ This glider is made in
Britain.

Children all around the world can make darts
and gliders from folding paper.
The art of folding paper was first developed
in Japan.

Wind toys - kites

Kites need the wind to fly in the air.
Kites are all shapes and sizes.

Kites need space to fly.
They can fly high and swoop and curl.
The long string moves and works the kite.

⬆ This is a Malaysian boy with his kite.

Children first played with kites in China.
The kites were made from thin paper or silk.
Nowadays kites are made from plastic.

Wind toys – hand windmills

Hand windmills turn round and round in the wind.

The first windmills came from
Holland and France.
They were made from wood.

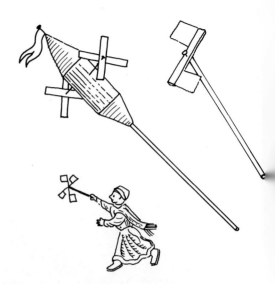

⬆ Nowadays hand windmills are made from plastic.

Glossary of words used in this book

Caterpillar wheels Caterpillar wheels help vehicles travel over bumpy ground.
They have a rubber or metal ring over two wheels.

Coconut shell A coconut shell is the outside of a large round nut
which grows in hot countries.

Festival A festival is a special time. People are happy and eat party food.

Kiwi A kiwi is a bird that lives in New Zealand

Mobile A mobile is a toy which can hang from the ceiling.
It moves about in the air.

Model A model is a small copy of something

Plastic Plastic is a strong, light material.
Plastic toys can be made in many different shapes.

Silk Silk is a fine, light cloth made from the thread of silkworms.

Spokes Spokes are the rods that go from the centre of a wheel to the rim.
They help the wheel keep its round shape.

Index

Countries toys come from

a b c d e f g h i j k l m n o p q r s t u v w x y z
A B C D E F G H I J K L M N O P Q R S T U V W X Y Z